i dream of peach seeds

fifty harvested poems:
2009-2019

by elias miller

Pretend Genius Press

London, New York, San Francisco, Seattle, Washington D.C.

Also available from Elias Miller:
Belt Loops and Bird Food

www.pretendgenius.com

Published simultaneously in the United States and Great Britain in 2019
by Pretend Genius Press
London, New York, San Francisco, Seattle, Washington D.C.

ISBN 978-0-9995277-5-7

To all those who were hobbled with shame,
who lived in the shadow of constant rain
who shot themselves when others took aim.

Contents

Preface

Only in my older years have the ideas of such prefaces gained purchase, otherwise I've tended to overlook them completely. I can say that now that I'm 50, I may occasionally have something interesting to say, or even more rarely, consider an idea to be wise. Most of the time, though, I still feel like I haven't got a clue. At least I'm wise enough to know that, finally.

Poetry is that love-hate desire I bury in the back yard for months at a time until, like a stubborn seed, it sprouts again with something verdant and disruptive, making me want to say things with layers of syncopation and rhythm. Like a pirate radio station, it encroaches on my frequency. It takes effort to hear these melodies and patterns, otherwise it just becomes feedback and static that clouds my mind. I've always liked similes and metaphors.

In my career doing years of computer work, computer meetings, computer monitoring, computer designs, computer malfunctions, computer malfeasance, computer rescues, computer insomnia, computer surprises, and computer meltdowns that create more computer meltdowns, this life has driven my creative side to distraction. Money: it makes me do "sensible" things. However, poetry is my vent that lets me still use my time for the required money-making part. I don't know what I would do if I wanted to write historical novels.

Another advantage of growing older is the desire to no longer deceive myself. I'm so tired now of avoiding the truth. Now if I could get over the compulsion to believe I can still fool others, I might actually be happier. I feel my potential achievements so far have been overshadowed by clouds of perpetual shame. I could be so much better than I am, but the shame defines itself and spreads itself forward (and sometimes backward) in time. The content of these poems are tinged with it. I don't know how to get beyond that yet, but for the time being I'm learning the value of distance, forgetfulness, and focusing on far more engaging things.

So kick back, grab a beverage, and enjoy these occasionally bitter literary fruits of the last decade. If nothing else, they can at least provide some reassurance that others struggle as well to make their way through the challenges of this thing we call life.

Elias Miller - October, 2019

i dream of peach seeds

listed

waterlines flowed street inclines
stop signs lined over white stripes
cracked tar filled cracks
acceleration pushed back into vinyl
bright sights flared through tinted glass
radio ads chattered
pacified strip malls
pasteurized marquis titles
simple leaves decayed in the open gutter

child sized hips and chipped strollers
car dents and powder mint paint jobs
black stone roads prone to expand
no sidewalks, only curbs
curved by plots of crabgrass and chickweed
the legal speed posted at forty-five
tires rolled unconsciously
holding tightly to steering wheels
high power lines crisscrossed gray cotton

mold dust swirled by a driveway push broom
booming sky explosions
cars clustered at the red line
revved by a rusted RV monolith
and a scuffed Arby's neon missing the 'y'
food wrappers, Styrofoam flowers
title pawns flashing dollar signs
magnification revealing green faults
designed to crumple under impact

shoulder clicks and bobbing necks
near wrecks by flares and flashing blue
giant-sized inflatable air dancers at rows of cars
trips to the far hill on fabric saddles and bar stools
cool breezes after winters numb
telling my skin what to think and do
these set pieces, turning points
alarm clocks struck dumb
dioramas separated by ropes and slow drinks

personal vectors intersected fender benders
snapshots cut into inconsequential sequences
like words in endless parallels that merge on the horizon
and spill in sudden cloudbursts from a bombastic sky

4/8/09

blind notes

he moves his baton by percussion and feel
syncopated notes in the orchestrated street scene
coda navigations, metronome curb taps
clear a path in the pedestrian flow

he knows what his skin knows
slow days in the sun hot face glow
television soundscapes
back to back mind shows with laugh tracks
stacked books he feels with fingertips
doorways, hallways, open windows
memorized steps, paces mapped
improvisational conversations with a cat
scatting in the dark house rows

he knows what his flesh knows
coffee steam rolls against his palm
stings of smoke in ember feelings
no dark or light, but the press of an evening
rolled into midnight shores
jazz notes, tympanic roars
waves of Parker, Gillespie, Navarro
familiar blankets
his sofa boat floating in the tidal draw

he knows the bruises, calluses
all knocks in the life stream
years of loose beats
sown into his inner eye
where pictures vibrate
shown textured, lightless
where bright heat buzzes and glows like skin
all part of the body of wisdom grown
inside his world of perpetual shadow.

7/31/09

3

When

I.

When August exhales heat in short gasps in the climax before September
When gym toned bottle blondes lead their dogs at sunset by a cell phone leash
When fecund oaks, acacia, aspen wrinkle leaf edges in a thousand soon to be goodbyes
When the sideways sun winks between branches as a jibe at the end of water play

When the lifeguard straightens deck chairs at dusk wearing a windbreaker, sucking a plastic whistle
When long hair and skateboards do horse-kicks and used moves to sneaker squeak ennui
When tennis courts stretch tar sealed backs in the cursive emptiness under elaborate chain link shadows
When clouds glow on the horizon like embers before inevitable black

When you wait for a tow on the roadside at sunset cracking knuckles and hoping for unplanned death
When the bedroom air is thick with stale pleas in the breaths after midnight suffocation
When mornings of harmonized mowers and blowers reverberate and die in the canals of autumn sleep-ins
When the day is divided, folded twice upon itself and left on your doorstep the next morning

When Caterpillars rust in the surveyed field with weeds growing over treads
When empty houses and lots dot like rotted teeth in the gaping mouth of the subdivision
When cleavage and legs vanish under clothing and nipples point at complete strangers
When yellow school buses flash red lights every block during the morning rush

When waistlines advance and hairlines slip at the inner seam of adulthood
When old cigarette butts are relit for one last bad drag at the emergency room door
When love and sex are cartoonish recollections replayed each evening before sleep
When liars and monsters read Salinger and Joyce in the coffeehouse sitting in the far corner under apartment wanted flyers with milk froth on their top lips

When Waffle House signs light up near lunchtime and fried breakfasts are served in the dark
When all cars drive in the same lines never passing, never looking back
When the same road signs point different ways depending on the time of day
When the perimeter road orbits a gray singularity at Little Five Points

When food is the only pleasure left leaving nothing but a husk of obesity
When youth is despised, resented and grieved for as you stream reruns of MTV
When windows only see into the past and walls are painted blue
When the sun warms the gooseflesh on your neck after pulling weeds before dusk

When all you buy is milk and beer in the corner store while holding a plastic bag
When anger and shame mix in even parts before the start of the conference call
When you stare in your rear view and only see the distant back of life
When you wait that extra moment with the radio off before leaving the car

When white walls and linoleum blankets invite you to stay for hours but never sleep
When all your friends keep electronic faces always smiling always right over your neck
When parents are absent, self-involved or dead
When telephones blink red hellos from unknown callers who want to collect

When words are sharpened and locked in drawers for future fights
When rainbows are only white light through rain at the recycling station
When muscles turn into fat and fat turns into remorse
When another day is spent watching seconds drain into coffee cups and dribble on your keyboard wrist rest

When there is melancholy in the wind and sorrow in the grass
When water fills the parking lot and chokes car clogged intersections
When the past is dead and the future unmakes itself before dinner
When apologies die and lips stay still in the minutes after your daughter's bedtime

When you walk to the car making sure we never touch
When you walk before neighbors making sure we do
When poetry and ugliness intertwine after perfunctory foreplay
When childhood forests are clear cut and familiar ground is stripped away

When screens get bigger and days get smaller
When new is the new old and old is the old new
When inspiration is dry and words are in short supply
When desire and disease are exactly the same and love is just a way to die

When days are watercolor strokes bleeding into gray
When children are washed away and parents are in jail
When the role models of today are only ghosts of men
When all that's left of when is now when now was only when.

II.
When thunderstorms, cobwebs, air conditioning, cold beds,
        skin dust, lunch hours, bus lines, tire treads,
                bumper stickers, cashed checks, traffic jams, bottlenecks,
                        soup diets, storm drains, forklifts, fatal wrecks,

global warming, plot twists, terror warnings, flu mist,
killer waves, rail crashes, drain cleaners, open graves,
leaf rakes, roof leaks, job ads, short weeks,
foreclosures, foreplay, fitness clubs, belly shakes,

                                monster masks, candy bags, diabetes,
                                cold sweat,
                                old fakes, ponzi schemes, credit scores,
                                terror threats,
                                burnt fuses, rolling blackouts, party
                                favors, play dates, bed sores, parent
                                nights, flight plans, red lights,

sack lunches,   whitening paste,   Sunday papers,   green waste,
road rage,   news breaks,   house paint,   tar shakes,

cake shows,   mortgage payments, late fees,   spinal aches,
black Fridays,   packing tape,   lake drives,   irish wakes,

odd jobs,
       party lines,
politicking,
       hard times,
sudden layoffs,
       magic tricks,
pot scrubbers,
       privileged whites,
air filters,
       Christmas lights,
pay freezes,
       face paints,
panty liners,
       walk-in pantries,
missile shields,
       raw steak,
eye candy,
       foaming cleaner,
dryer sheets,
       derelicts,
dead babies,
       door stops,
buzz cuts,
       gummy snakes,
          camouflage,
            brain traumas,
               sound bites,
                  birthday cakes,
                    sound offs,
                       chiropractors,
                 air mattress,
             railroad tracks,
          script meetings,
       sex scandals,
     air bags,
    pricing checks,
coupon codes, fighter jets,
siren warnings, microwaves,
cell plans, clothing sales,
gas prices, crowded jails,

grass seeds, empty shelves,
axle grease, pay scales,
dead fathers, holy sons,
splintered families, lost pens,

6

glass shards,
band-aids,
Catholic guilt,
used Zen,
scapegoats,
plastic sporks,
drama queens,
straw men
are all that's left of when.

III.
When the when was when was when was now
Was then the when of when
Now and then when you call
Is when I think of when
The when that when was all before
Before the when of then
After all the whens before
Instead of at the end
When all that's left of when is now
When now was only when.

10/6/09

Picture this

I slide into frame
A sway by this apple tree
I say
It's all you need
Your fingers splayed
Red hand
Arrested

I say
Take

He is naked
You are naked
It rains and you both shiver

Our three reflections ripple
Above the growl of your new hunger

10/14/09

passed off

in young days
you dropped a snow globe
slow-mo fall off the table
fractals and coastlines
fine shards and glass
refracted in sunlight

glitter fell in cracks
ocean drives
backed by Pacific cliffs
sea mist
seagulls glide
tidal pools accumulate

remember the ways
you memorized dioramas
colored mosaics
your sand castles erode
static waves just
wash, rinse, repeat

get yourself together
get cleaned up
set pieces spilled
swept
all filed in your attic

life is as long as a snowfall

10/14/09

Welcome Home

Striped in red white blue
His child floated above them
The Hercules' glided descent
Men lined in rows on the tarmac
Stiff breathing, starch pressed,
Star buttons reflected the sun.

After salutes in duplicate, triplicate
Box in hand, pockets empty
Dad took him home to plant him
By the tree where he broke his collar bone
By the streets where he rode without training wheels
Into the hole of silence and memory.

10/20/09

A Buk Pose

Things are quiet today
Across from the server room
People walk by
Say "Hello,
How's it going."
I always say "Fine" or "Good"
Because that's all people want to hear
When they walk by.

My office is close to the kitchen
Smells of coffee and trash
Congregate around my desk

I have two monitors:
One has this poem on it
The other has a tech website
White walls
Hums of the server fans
Fluorescent lights
Wood grain Formica
These are my day's surroundings

No windows
Pipes and air vents overhead
Sounds of the warehouse
Forklifts
Shouts
The occasional break into song
This is the way my workday is long
As I sit in this cave
And try to create
Some daylight

10/21/09

the last Texan

he used to say the world had eaten him
those final evenings in front of the projection TV
dinner cooling on a wooden meal tray
memories of Lubbock days
penny movies, painted twilights
pulling ragweed from his mother's brick planter boxes
rootworm captives cooked by a magnifying glass

he saved old string, popsicle sticks
used them for guns and magic swords
played war with four brothers
always wearing his red cowboy hat
nimble runs through nutsedge, crabgrass
fallowed paddocks not far from the cemetery
and the fresh Amarillo clay of his father's grave

long limbed walks to the Brazos with stick fishing poles
navigated pock-marked roads, ruddy faces
segregated shakes at Pinson's drug store.
before long he made his attempts at manhood
crashing the family Dodge Deluxe before the prom
but back then he was scrawny and simple
with frequent dates and streaks of pomade

he trekked out of Texas with imprecision
infantry in Okinawa, masters in Colorado
teaching physics in Oahu between beach swims and sunburns
finally landing in San Francisco fog and hippiedom
Lubbock receded in his rear view along with his twang
leaving two forgotten marriages and two forgotten sons
then a female student became this final one

thirty years on and little to show
gray photos of a lost cowboy
his ukulele broken and stored on the bookshelf
boxes of dry ball points and always his bits of string
a collection of Starbucks coffee rings
done crosswords folded, nine down
an eight-letter word for irrevocably.

11/5/09

<u>reborn</u>

do you remember my reply, one finger parallel to the sky?
- The Shins

you were reborn in the bathtub at the Comfort Inn
Denver snow blanketing details
scrub and sagebrush forgotten until the thaw
blue skies drawn on cinder blocks
white capped flat rooftops
burlap clouds blowing fine dust

you fell out and slid on white tiles
eyes open for the first time
thin towels out of reach
mirror fogged except for the corner near the heat lamp
worn paperback half soaked, moved by the door
slow steam rose from shaking limbs

you heard vacuums drone down the hall
though the TV played 80s' music
Split Enz, the Police, New Order, the Cure
regressions of your past life soundtrack
Ray Bans, pegged pants and flat top cuts
always looking for a date sometime in the future

no doctors were there to suture the tear
you swayed on rubbery legs
swaddled and stumbled into bed
head peaked, fontanel open
wrapped poly-cotton sheets, blackout curtains
hiding the high plains desert softened by snow

I never fully considered the postpartum
the moment I told you where to go.

11/17/09

march of the shadow men

he died under his white Dodge Caravan
arms black wedged in the engine bay
unable to pay a mechanic to replace the part
he left the starter hanging by one bolt

having already drained the transmission
cardboard padded the grainy driveway
he changed the radiator fan relay for his wife's PT
the man (made of honey-do) scanned the toolbox for a spanner

yesterday the front yard, raked and swept
black bags stowed behind the neighborly high hedge
upstairs vacuumed, bathrooms cleaned
he meant to cut up the branch pile from the spring

he had one beer between jobs and whistled a bit
used the blower to clear the back deck
his daughter ran to the neighbors to play
two minutes before the Dodge crushed his neck

and though his watch said ten to three
those dark hands smearing his face
no longer applied, the job though half-done
would be left to another man in another place

and the Caravan would move again
leaves raked by other hands other days
his space filled by shadow men
arms black wedged in the engine bay.

12/2/09

RIP in Chuck E Cheese

in booth 4c by the projector screen
red shirt waiters wait for me to finish
pizza dishes litter laden tables
as Coke and crumbs dribble my shirt folds

kids jump and twirl on the sticky carpet
while Chuck E sings his mechanized routine
conversations jostle, bump and rebound
video game sounds back the cries for mommy mommy

Skeeball clashes with basketball shots
hot flashing neon, canned applause
syndicated logos, syncopated static
Buffalo wings smeared by chocolate frosting

kids push in line, jostle in place
stealing turns, whining cries
harmonies vie with speaker feedback
rock beats and solo screams

babies in arms stuff money into cash boxes
and tickets spit out like unrolling tongues
play structures masticate children
while i slip down the plastic bench seat

Mr. Cheese greets a mob of marked hands
as heart throbs slow, roll
an undertow pulls at my feet, dark echoes
hold my head sideways to see two eyes glare

a silent stare, awkward steps away
a set of pigtails points
then runs off to play.

12/9/09

Mongolian Steps

in the month of Tavdugaar Sarr when the grass regrew
precious weeks before he knew her name
he footed up the hillside from Soviet concrete
from the small criss-cross of uneven streets
and smelled summer rolling down the undulations

he survived dry winter and the dust storms of spring
feeding on potatoes, ramen, boiled lamb
his days marked out in Russian dubs of 80's TV
snacking on canned crab he found at the State store
at times lying still on the floor to straighten his back

he scoured ad hoc markets of Chinese counterfeit goods
dodged del-wearing drunks as they slurred "Russkii"
avoided the green snot spat on cracked sidewalks
weekly washed his clothes by hand in the bathtub
and swallowed salted milk tea as a courtesy

but that day the skirt hem of warmth beckoned
he left his apartment block to walk past wildflowers
watched small herds of furry horses drink from streams
and lost the city in the verdant folds of the khedeh
the bosom of the land that nursed Genghis' army

in those still minutes, he asked a question
not thinking it would be heard or even listened to
two larks flew past him down towards food
the sky stared blue with a blink of white
sunshine glowed equally on everything in sight

then as he descended back towards town
four smoke stacks pointed out of green cleavage
red printed numbers on each digit
like a countdown.

12/16/09

<u>this white girl</u>

she was always called a white girl
translucent tracks mapped thin legs
the sight of awkward birthmarks hidden
she wore no shorts outside her home

Celtic roots, she frequently saw red
flashes of violence and wall dents
tensed arms that longed to hold
but more than not pushed us away

she initially faired well with men
her children all tanned, brown haired
she sought the company of dark angels
below the shadow of the Salvation Cross

her Southland British twang stood out
and salty words seasoned her banter
thirsty, she drank too much for the taste of love
often draining a bitter cup

she sang constant hymns in the kitchen
while unpeeled potatoes boiled in the pot
watching for answers in misleading impulses
repeated in time on the flat screen

I used to say I knew her
she once tasted like home
before frustration twisted us
and showed us to be strangers

She said I was never man enough
repeated with wringing chaffed and crooked hands
plans, broken plans, impossibilities
she baked one last batch of heavy brownies

head askew
she opened green windows
feeding the squirrels with whole peanuts
while off-key humming "Hallelujah".

1/06/10

Northwestern Qiblih

at Christmas, Allah's underpants will express
Koranic retribution strapped in cotton
virgin loins prejudiced, dispense
quick hot death via explosive modalities

questions translated lose angels
years alone he serenaded
"my love, my love, raise your skirt,
connect me in dreadful concupiscence!"

wet dreams whet his inelegant eyes
adolescent breaths, fumbled grasps
bury dark thoughts barely
arms reached skyward, piercing air

all heathen planes fly at midnight
as Allah clutches his pocket watch.
airborne death to Western heresies
who am i to explain why?

1/19/10

ashes

The shrieking of nothing is killing, just pictures of Jap girls in synthesis...
- David Bowie

with hot thorns you digressed early
hunted by charges dressed in words
urges burned white in your five points
but you paced damp suburban cul-de-sacs
hand-clenched steps made forgotten tracks

icicles clutched at thick rooftops
worn snow angels laced with smoke
missing one knit glove, a red crumpled hole
swollen breasts, burning openings
you lunged at restraint and moaned like a whore

in sordid constructions covered by brick
you shut the storefront and forced a smile
gritting through another hungry moment
like windows braced against a storm
salivation flowed from tongues like orchids

you exhaled lungfuls until cold
this time held back, older and greyer,
your hot air rolled up in plumes
black steam, gold hue, because
you never did anything out of the blue

2/17/10

riders

a short man struts
face tats and tattered sweats
carries his chip across the station lobby

single moms chase small ones
young bloods pull up pants
college backpacks strap plus-sized honeys

I'm living fewer lies
at 2am on grated benches
with goodbyes to my once friend

not yet reached the end of line
riders huddle, wait and circulate
grey sleeper sideways takes two seats

creased foreheads greased by nicotine smells
heavy eyes outline tile floors
smokers quell cold in a two-step outside

it's nothing I haven't seen before
derelicts, family splinters, the poor
roving at all hours in all directions

we queue again boarding northward
tired and sagging flesh pressed
fresh from the Greyhound station

some of us two seat corpulent
others grizzled skeleton thin
old hairlines, wisps of youth

we ride again on our ways
broken sleep transmitting like Morse code
a broadcast into anonymous night

3/7/10

<u>in the shower I remember God</u>

alone in Siberia living in a dorm
I slept where deep window sills kept food cold
people moaned their codes through thick walls
old thoughts echoed, Soviet with despair
my breathing rose and dispersed into nowhere

dark snow on once roads, broken vodka crates
loads of potatoes sold, bread like bricks
gold-teethed drunkards stumbled under street lamps
gangs of then school kids fought in a jumble
patrons jostled me and mumbled "get lost, Georgian."

my sole pleasure was the basement showers
I wore flip flops and mold covered green tiles
but the water was near searing and I showered alone
a traveler at midnight under hot clean rain
the day's stains stopped and I was new again

I was never especially kempt
but I learned to love the God of cleanliness
to this day I praise Him and His small pleasures
during times of winter teeth and frozen air
when my steam rose and dispersed into nowhere.

3/24/10

The Quiet Car

At dawn the quiet car rolls on black ribbons
Red stars paired in rows stare pinholes
Charts pale courses on cold curves
Sole steering holds my own direction
Treads tracing old arguments down parallel roads

The sun glow is only from dust blown
Above foothill peaks in motion relief
Slow rowboat ripples after the oar lifts
The horizon flows, a seamless argument
Standing signs rise to punctuate monotones

This open highway pulls like a shoelace
And I follow, destination unseen tracing white lines
Above the Denny's sign the day star wavers and is gone
And the sky, erased, waits for birds or a plane
While my engine growls as I accelerate.

5/14/10

Parking Lot

One square mile of asphalt pressed
Divided by white lines like a math test
Car-less dark echoes the sound of crickets
As Carrie Underwood glows coiffed on the buzzing marquis

My keys hang from the steering column
I watch them huddle behind tinted glass
The last cars pass, blinders on, slight pause
Ballet dresses point from the back seat and are gone

Mercury lights die so I see a star or two
Pinpricks through the damp blanket of fog
Growing conifers just shadows against the sky
And I am the last stranger, hand glowing, awaiting rescue.

6/18/10

17 Years

Sunday you walk the painted curb
the smell of downtown dumpsters linger
by outside racks of an unnamed store
your clothes hang like fallen drapes
her eyes don't notice you anymore

she has no closeness to the sea
but in vacant lots, you imagine shore
garbage waves wash broken glass
swirls of dust and stinging spray
the hard flow traffic roar

her subway entrance takes you down
41 steps to underground decor
recycled air and fluorescence shakes
these sighs no longer make you warm
red lights flash, soundless signs

days pass measured out in rail-cars
tunnels penetrated reach far into veins
steel trains vibrate hard seats and sore hamstrings
she shows what she wants you to see
dark walled vistas and flashed stops on the way

and this day you rise from the ground
the sound of engines revving, random horns
daylight blinding pale-skinned blinks
morning papers blown regaling her minutiae
from shop windows, sun-bleached displays

the city exhales smoke and smiles
her yellow fog circles skyscrapers grown
miles of roads and jumbled tracks crisscrossed
her back arches and is lost in a stretch
a sleepless pose from her bed of stone.

8/14/10

<u>my abused</u>

you've had two years two years to wait
each daylight made a separate life
my reminder hiding upstairs, upstairs
gaining fine lines, divine heels,
vampire fangs out ready to bite

you've had two years two years confused
and to clarify to clarify and and
i don't dry dry tears
my hungers stalk behind bars and bars
when i see you near, walk by lingering

you've had two years two years to salivate
sleeping with him, dogs at your feet
leashes mated to your agile hands
his demands lain like a plea, pleas,
their bodies decayed under painted floors

you've had two years to my forty-two
so approach me, don't approach
this clenched love takes all fortitude
on floral bed sheets worn and used
please please do, do not, refuse

and abuse me my sweet abused.

9/14/10

I take you in

From pink peach toenails to a still hazel gaze
From leg-shaped jeans ending in gilded soles
From the thin grey sweater draped over crossover arms
From straight strands pulled back to display high cheek bones
From these beauty spots placed like random punctuation
From your prone leopard-skin handbag carry-on
From pressed lips dried in recirculated subway air
From blonde hair and brunette roots
From the way you fold in the plastic chair
From the days of forgotten affairs and afternoons in poolside glory
From coffee sipped and old novels read Friday nights at the Flying Biscuit
From dead conversations with mom about former boyfriends and fall fashion
From younger sisters who always get what they want when they want it
From college friends and college enemies in forefront Facebook drama
From plans of conquest and the flat press against glass ceilings
From short skirts, closed legs and open toes
From shaded examinations across an empty car
From train riders who ignore you and others who stare
From your constant finger grip on your careless male shield
From your smile always understated always there
From the transition of your shoulders to your rounded chin
From the steam which rises from your forehead before coffee breaks
From the arched back walks made on parade heels
From sticky flirtations and spray on skin
From dance floor hookups and hotel-stay intimacies
From go-go dancers and rainbow shooter trays
From the stretched neck ennui of unasked for delays
From statements of blue Adidas and white socks standing in line
From pregnant silence to aborted thoughts
From the soft mouth clutching a sharp tongue
From magic moments when lights are cut to the press of the first kiss
From memories of cops and robbers and jails in the jungle gym
From Sundays of God, wine and wafer lip service
From stifled sighs in the tired moments touched on before dreams
From the occasional sleep-ins and breakfasts of cornflakes and ice cream
From folded skin and slippery moisturizing routines
From cell phone distractions in the last three metro stops
From days on the rag watching repeats of the OC
From circular thoughts and a modern repudiation of traditional logic
Form wordless goodbyes and silent hellos
From quick examinations before his pen writes again
From sideways gravity and involuntary rocking at the lullaby end of the line

26

From the points of consciousness that connect in questionable constellations
From waxed legs and the application of shaded foundation
From the fear of wrinkles and the dissections of random strangers
From impatience and complaints in the afternoons spent with absent daddy
From stolen after-school cigarettes and air freshener deceptions
From the first kiss-ups to the last piss-ups
From the last time spent across from someone you will never met
From everything thin and straight, everything soft and curved
From detailed shadings to broad brush strokes
From clean ideals to dirty lines
From complexities to caricatures
From generalities to specificities
From hard truth to plain platitudes
I take you in

I take you in
And spit you out
I can only take in so much.

9/29/10

<u>turn this page</u>

she said she swam out into the sea
but it wouldn't take her down
washed on sand like brown kelp
breaths sighed with jellyfish feelers
drowned at the side of the crime-scene beach

her orange halves on a china plate
her orange stars round a circle moon
she wore apples on her dress
pressed into visions of orchards
flapping in the wind before the storm

she stepped stone streets in thin heels
gray dawns lain in solo beds
cold meals, day old bread
once he left she said she was free
and God spoke through her fingertips

her bottle poured its wisdom
her bottle emptied words
glasses stole syllables from the throat
churned into novels conjured in pubs
thrown out in alleys and spilled on lost curbs

she said I took her line
traced in vertebrae curved, vertebrae arched
she finds me amusing when I lie
arguments spent, the sweat of debate
made to conclude late conversations

"wait" I voiced before morning
before her end of stolen days
she kissed my knuckles in sequence
fake reverence, she laughed at ten
and spoke, "you gave me no choice"

so along with these fingers, her lips
pronouncements fade in forgetful skin
only dried remnants of breakfast remained
inscribed and missed on the plate
a testament signed on an unlined page.

10/4/10

BP

Your words burst on the surface after days of flame and smoke
No boats dare approach to skim or hold them back
This black brown scar floats, coating horizons
You choke everything in sight
Then pause to light a low-tar slim
No luck, your monologue starts again
Something about a pipe being broken

You're done you're done you're done
You spew, devout cameras review real-time
While scientists and movie stars scout your unbound slick
Sick gulls and sea turtles dip in dish soap and are nursed
Resort owners and fisherman spit collective curses
Two lovers tiptoe in wetlands near your crude line
They say you even poison sand until it forgets time

Nights pass beneath these false black ceilings
Snaking track-lights project brightness in cones
Fliers, posters, layered like worn wallpaper
I say I'm out and about, but still alone
Staring through backwards shop-window writing
A coffee-toned street scene, cars drone by
Waiters clean tables to say goodnight goodnight.
I am not ready to go.
But the edge of the stretch of the end is here
Soon I will be outside
In the night that hides faces, uneven strides,
Locked storefronts dividing open spaces
Quadratic places sizing mismatched blocks

They say BP is systolic diastolic
Each beat surging in locked pipes underneath
Only lost when there's a blow-out
Pressures release years of ancient sediment
Your sentiments, bare, just stretched stains on watery skin
First gushed like death in uncontrolled thick spray
When everything that held us exploded and finally fell away.

11/03/10

Long Division

In the lines of long seconds at the business stall
Your music fades, not real at all, just discrete reminders
Kisses once flesh, now digitized memory
Chemical triggers flash, old habits,
I sip a cup of corporate coffee

You shed another layer of skin I used to touch
Dark spots appear and disappear
A piano plays a ballad from the binary speaker

This winter cold is just a tilt of earth
We rotate as we should, sometimes wobbling
Some future day, we are closer to the sun
Though our moon still moored
And we will rise from our yoga balls and indoor workouts
Baring our limbs at the waterline of opposite shores
(Cue Adele - Cold Shoulder)

Let us document this divide
Submit forms, make calls, reply, forward,
Coffee stimulates, music players on randomize
Your music fades, not real at all, just virtual reminders
In the lines of long seconds at the business stall

1/28/11

#1020

She has an ottoman like a lotus
where Ganesh could have put up his legs
sporting Stanford sweats she circulates seamlessly
the single bedroom apartment her tidy diorama
cool sky blues and metrosexual browns counterbalance
she moves towards me looking at my mouth
and I slide into the space she makes with her smile

Toffee skin curves under the white duvet
she presses into me and runs fingers over my palm
we talk noses touching, eyes open halfway
with frequent kisses and close words
forgetting boundaries, barriers hidden away
I breathe in her sighs and ask the question
she replies, "this is only an island."

her parents' young faces framed gaze from the mantle
she clicks on the LCD to watch March Madness
college students cheer over hyperbolic commentators
"These are my people," she says, minding the remote
I move to her doorway, laptop bag shoulder-draped
she steps in for the last smile and kiss
as I trace the arch of her back until she pulls away
and I'm nudged into the corporate-trimmed hallway.

4/5/11

Cast away

You wrap me up in striped canvas
tan digits clench below duvet waves
the ceiling fan spins, a naked propeller
there beside the flailing crush of sheets
Hindu gods extend red arms
your bronze coating twists and goes under
invitations lost as quickly as found
an ocean of space suddenly opens up.

You don't believe in supply in demand
and favor specifics over tales
not being an academic I flounder
preferring kisses to statistics
(quiet moments are rarely calculated)
but in the end, you say math doesn't lie
fazed by the uncertainties of our warm bodies
almost moving in parallel, once touching for hours

In my dreams you are a lotus unfolding
petals graphed as interconnected curves
floating tossed on an ocean back
currents pull you out of reach
until the sun rises and I am alone
an orange raft clinging to blue skin
rolling in unpredictable certainties

4/21/11

the booth

she leans on elbows in the red vinyl booth
chrome trimmed Formica table
napkin dispensers blurred with grease
the town outside a dusty painting
backwards writing blocking the skyline
her time, just a pose
in a flower dress
waiting for repose.

jacket sleeves too short
old clothes scuffed and torn
he knows he's almost late
owned by the road, miles-worn shoes
subtract distance to the day's close
an awning or doorway
maybe a cold grass field
or other places of unflinching prose

it takes a moment for time to regrow
she thinks unselfconsciously as the pie arrives
the waitress fakes a wrinkled smile
and slides the signed check sideways
flowered dress reflects on her nail before the plate
unearthly cherries rest
sliced in red halves by the knife
buried in sheets of buttered dough

it's been days since old clothes was told
the letter folded in his left pocket
his legs asking, "to know, to know?"
calculations of rudimentary math
running outcomes and scenarios
his ruddy dome shines
sun beating down the road
as he approaches the center of town

a cigarette, her sole foe
she consoles herself taking a puff
plaid diners and solo moms, children in tow
an old friend's folded note said to wait
after the wake and the flow of guests
her time, just a pose

in a flower dress
waiting for repose

past the rusted goalposts of the football field
he steals down side streets to right road
the diner wedged between True Value and a closed cinema
he holds the side of an old lightpost
flowered dress displays in the window
smoke ribbons on her face rising slow
none of her coiffed hair out of place
Hopper might have painted her there

cars and bodies pass, the filter on her lips
then a lack of motion catches her eye
a homeless guy listing against a post
ragged clothes, splitting shoes, jacket too small
a high forehead reflects the sun
eyes fixed on hers
and she holds his gaze for seconds
then looks down at her pie

she is grown from the far past
a laughing child in the open yard
flowered dress flowed in summertime
vague feelings of her hand as they walked to the fair
too much he missed
after the last hug and cheek kiss
he stares for a minute before he turns away
perhaps some bench is waiting for him

flowered dress looks up through smoke and he is gone
the codger must have wised up and moved on
her pie feels thick and tasteless like the day
wasted minutes never to replay
she leans on elbows, unfolds the note
her time, just a young girl's pose
in a flower dress
waiting for repose

4/27/11

Poetry Redux

Eyes heavy from the way I've tried to please
My words ingratiate me, grate me
My soul seized by a secondary purpose
Yoked to no one in particular
Yet visceral, aimless
Of whatever impulse comes to the surface

Today I see how soft I've become
The mirror outlines me in new ways and old fears
My mind bigger than all of this
Restless, unsatisfied, bristling
I survey the day and see no escape
Nothing I wear fits anymore

This is my consequence, my result
Disconnected, lazy, never becoming
Half-developed hopes, unfinished endings
My rudder stuck, engine sputtering
Course set in circles of consequence
Because because because because

Of whatever impulse comes to the surface
Yet visceral, aimless
Yoked to no one in particular
My soul seized by a secondary purpose
My words ingratiate me, grate me
I'm tired of the way I've tried to please.

9/10/12

When there is nothing left to say

When there is nothing left to say
Cubicle desks lay open faced
Office chairs tucked neatly away
Simulated woodgrain displays, "naturally"

When there is nothing left to say
Cars abandon raised freeways
Neighborhood streets, new parking lots
Intersections in recent memory

When there is nothing left to say
Swings barely sway in shiftless air
Sandpiles shrug off blurry footprints
And long for the open sea

When there is nothing left to say
Bed sheets stretch crisp and plain
Your whited canvas drying, waiting
My outline, a negative space

When there is nothing left to say
Phone calls fill with practiced refrains
Words make walls from bridges razed
And greetings translate to "Stay away"

When there is nothing left to say
We become skilled at measurement, data
Tipping scales in our favor, equations
Until we solve for x, and x we become

When there is nothing left to say
We are new strangers in an old land

When there is nothing left to say
We know all and understand no one

When there is nothing left to say
This is the end.

10/01/12

36

Please Ask Me

You are under my skin on days when you do nothing
Your fingers feel me from inside
Tracing nerves, dendrites
Reading my thoughts as they stream in

Blood moves for you, hot cheeks, cold hands
Hair brushes strands against arteries, veins
Tangled in your reins, you bend me
To the least of your ends, a willing beast

I am man, half-man saddled with hunger, ache
Caged and pacing I stalk you within
Trapped in your fate, your tight non-embrace
I face you, raw desire pleading to satiate

In your casual stare across your leg
A single look will make me beg.

7/23/13

Demolition

Something is broken in love
And longing to be broken remains
Long after we are finished
And drained of emotion.

Love is the destroyer
And I am ready to be remade.

8/4/13

The Long Goodbye

To KL – I was more paralyzed than you ever were

The day you decided to die, i had no words
i forced myself to talk in the meeting room
facing a tan corner next to the fake fichus
hot tears wiped away

The day you decided to die, i had to work
people asked me pointless questions
i smiled and joked
as grief burned in multiple organs

The day you decided to die, i disconnected
i fed, drank and made merry
irish madness for the sake of your pre-death
mourning the morning countless days before your wake

The day you decided to die, cruelty came to visit
and stayed up all night playing Black Sabbath
until he punched my wall saying
"That's all buddy."

The day you decided to die, waves reached my feet
and retreated, sand sucked away and i faltered
while thinking something stupid
about horizons and sunsets

The day you decided to die, i crushed up poems
and threw away all forms of beauty
or at least a piece thereof
it was all pompous bs anyway

The day you decided to die,
i decided, i decided i decided
did i really need to decide? Yes love,
i had to decide you already died.

12/26/13

<u>my whole existence is flawed</u>

i spoke too much, smoking a camel on the porch
much too much you repeat, such a shame
a sham, i elaborate. but i came too late to apologize
the rain pours over the side of the blocked grate
atlanta shrugs, smug humidity
it wears me out to be fake all the time
if i could be
if i could be, you refrained
you always had my way with words.

when it's late and the moon is just a toenail clipping
i sit shirtless and think of you on a dark divan
somewhere a shadow drapes an arm
drawn into your diorama
i pull the curtain and watch the drama
paid for your lessons
your lessons you said
you learned from the best
dressed in my t-shirts and your torn stockings

i'll be forever in your debt you said
the rain tapering, puddles clapping
i know the denouement is soon at hand
i'll mend i said, having spoken too much
my camel smoked to the butt end
bent and soaked on the wet porch
it wears me out
it wears me out, you refrained
you always had my way with words

5/13/14

The Ice Storm

It rained ice in Atlanta overnight
water freezing on naked trees
crystalline twigs glowing in street lights
chattered in the night wind chill
breezes blew right through clothing
layers now building under my skin
I can't help feeling slowly snowed-in.

I don't sleep. It's been months since you verbalized
in the unheated café on Ponsonby
leather pockets stiff in July
there is nothing there is nothing
upside down in our conversation
but the cold broke me, ice cut
memorized speeches designed
divined into attempts divided
I tried I tried
and it was the least you could do, least
inclined to make any sort of move beyond the superficial
and dive into the betrayal and heartache
once and for all break the bonds that held you back.

I have no knack with spoken words
my lips drift above my soul
but my fingers my fingers connected can explain
(even though I cracked them from age 9)
they give my circumstance flesh and meaning.
I could be reading this to a crowd
waiting for the mandatory clap
but I would prefer you slapped me or connected
right cross left
shouted with spittle
sputtered with incoherent stuttered accusations
you you did this you did this!
but instead iron chairs sucked heat from our bodies
and we stayed only until leaving
awkward pauses in our cadence
scraping metal feet on concrete floors.

This morning, white sleet glazed tree lines
trunks supine in forced humility
icicles clung like clear bindings

41

drawing down branches, splitting fault lines
lying at their feet like an offering
my arms extended, they almost bend
as I wait I wait for a thaw.

2/26/15

Catch up

i planned to write this for you
surreptitious verse a vis
purple stockings and thick heels
risk averse glasses
cottage cheese ceilings

that was the 90s you said
when Nirvana still echoed
and college slowed to a trickle
you rode a blue moped
sold time for pizza and sweat

i was not just bleeding
i bled for thistle, rosemary, dill
still, i made better dishes
you laughed with bare teeth
lipstick smeared on white

i never turned out lights
when i fumbled, never unclasped
unzipped, my lips searching
pursed against your question
i was just stupid and young

you sigh over the phone
wireless vibes wash through sunlight
i'm tired, i tried, i tied
knots knowing nothing, your sweater
unbuttoned, t-shirt light
untucked, soft under fingers, your words

stuck, you were not my first
but i liked you.

3/11/15

<u>my poetry is gone</u>

my poetry is gone, his bottle is empty
tapping it repeatedly only gives drops,
the dross of language, he drunk walks
wearing just black socks on cold feet

my poetry is gone, he took the last train
leaving only one shoe and a musical note
under a squeaky floorboard in the sleeper car
a guitar strummed "oh suzannah"

my poetry is gone, he kicked the bucket
and buried himself in the midwest
under anonymous tumbleweeds and hard scrub
after vultures picked clean his carcass

my poetry is gone, he took the freeway
evading authorities for hours
until he sideswiped a school bus
and was subdued on foot with a taser

my poetry is gone, he fled to mexico
in the back of dusty taqueria truck
where he now siestas on a beach
beside sand scorpions and warm margaritas

my poetry is gone, he was vaporized
by a cruise missile meant for ISIS
the army apologized, two officers arrived
and said it was only friendly fire

my poetry is gone, he got lost in the library
wandering the philosophy stacks
somewhere between CAM 190.204 and CAN 190.305
leaving duodecimal fingerprints in the dust of a forgotten card catalog

my poetry is gone, he escaped from maximum security
through an underground tunnel on a dirt bike
up a ladder to a construction site
where he gave me the finger and skidded away on his motorcycle

my poetry is gone, he vanished in the bayou
after a manhunt through the mangroves

as police dogs barked throughout
and gators slid cleverly into dark water

my poetry is gone, he was shot into space
to orbit with satellites and exotic debris
where he watched weather patterns
and spied on the military moves of north koreans

my poetry is gone, he grew up and went to college
where he pledged a fraternity and spent two years
drinking beer and dating coeds
before being expelled for academic malfeasance

my poetry is gone, he became anonymous
and processed spreadsheets in cubicles
only phoning the IT department when printing stopped
for the ranks of pressed shirts and corporate automatons

my poetry is gone, he was only a lark, a soupçon,
a thought bubble that popped
as it floated in the ocean of consciousness
and amused some sharks before he fled

my poetry is gone, oh my poetry is gone
but his collar said "if found please return"
so come home to me you old hound,
your worn leash is waiting.

1/12/16

the last ride

when my high horse dies
i'll finally see you sunken, hungry
eyes on some former timeline
waiting to be eaten on the inside
the cries of children rise from the far room

when my high horse dies
swollen skies will rip on a white steeple
pouring water beside your final beard
the grey light flooding your grey box
to drown your downsized appetite

when my high horse dies
your carriage will arrive in red mud
red hands carrying you slightly
your concrete demise propped as we revise you,
dogs at your feet writhing as we eulogize

when my high horse dies
it implies there's some kind of insight
when old prides are buried
itemized, and scrutinized after tears have dried
their logistics now summarized into someone else's hanging files

when my high horse dies
i'll reside in the rectangle dug by the excavator
worms and flies will invite themselves in
i won't mind when i remember your reply
the last time i rode into the horizon.

4/14/16

home(in)stead

when the radio played your favorite song
i sang it too, the engine hummed along
your details reduced to some temporal vanishing point
but i still remember music as rubber and tarmac
rolled me towards a known horizon

your words once filled the rear seat, the boot,
some strapped to the roof rack
there was barely enough space for me
but i carried them for years
like a homeless person in their car
with hardly room to see out back
if i took a turn too hard
words toppled in my lap
saying, "drive slower, moron"
and i would return them to their biased stack

the world is tied in black ribbons
black smoke, rising tides
i said i'd dive into the coast
where i was born, on windy beaches
gripped with ice plants, arctic currents,
cracked stones beaten down so small
they can be walked over and washed away
i missed the bridges and the bay
the choke of rush hours and dirty rain
young faces stretched and grown
grey memories holding to older bones

i carried your millstone this far
back to uneven roads, crossroads
the folds of brown hills bolted down with tract homes
continuous strip malls in the baked tar-seal sea
i crossed the country to return to something
and in the end it isn't much
a glimpse of neighborhood familiarity
where your words lose their veracity
in the vagaries of old definitions
when i was too young and blind to be free.

5/9/16

when death comes

when death comes, she'll send a singing telegram
with worn tap shoes and a run in her fishnet stockings
pausing for an awkward tip after the final denouement

when death comes, my legs will buckle in the office
tipping the water cooler, and smashing salted vending machine snacks
my manager will file a comp report with corporate HR

when death comes, signs in the sky will flash like roadside billboards
showing only Newport cigarette ads, nostalgic whiskey bottles,
and the salvation signs of "Got Jesus?"

when death comes, he'll knock three times before putting his foot in my door
and sign me up for one hundred unwanted magazine subscriptions

when death comes, a slow love song will play in the background
saying it's always watching as i sway along

when death comes, i'll drive fast in the desert, windows open, arms flapping,
while the wind waters my eyes and cracks my panting lips

when death comes, the flood will wash all cube farms away
and locusts will strip the corporate greenway

when death comes, i'll try to recite Whitman, Ginsberg or Frost
but words will be lost in a choke of white angels

when death comes, you'll play Radiohead, Bauhaus and other dark songs
and I'll draw a cartoon skulls and bones

when death comes, i'll finally forget about me
and eternity will replace my memories.

when death comes, it'll just be a drive-by.

5/24/16

We Belong

It's a Friday and Pat Benitar plays
The office shuffles papers and taps on keys
Felt tips wet, roller-balls prepped
Louvered windows shade springtime days

the earth is crust on a boiling stone
hot and cold convulsions clapping thunder metronomes
corruptions of nature roam free
giving life, stealing life in pay-to-play slavery
systems of civility, barbarity
carnivorous assets, dark assembly lines
orchard lines, crop lines
define lifetimes of no higher purpose
cultivations of such false inclines bear bitter fruit
hands in peat, manure, clutching worms
clutching paper, clutching cheap oil creations
defaulting term loans into prison uniforms
making craters and sink holes, burning rivers
gassing faucet explosions, fracking us
exactly the way they want us to be
as we slough off refinement, precision and return
to more primal modalities
hands on a rock, a club, a colored rag
tribalizing heterogeneity into component factions
digital veils just fractions, facets of truth
raised to shield, not shield the glare of indigenous disparity
the earth is not a mother
but a cold shoulder, a wanton whore
of half-breeds, abominations and seething procreations
how should we walk in suits to our suburban artifices
but backwards in time to the truth of our simplicity
reducing order to more archetypal brutality
order? not the rule of the day
but impulses to slay, take and pray
to the god of the searing day and freezing night
blood on altars and burnt offerings, the pinnacle of our plea
please please please
pronounce us mad and make us back into clay
cosmic hands, crush us, mold us
compress us into gray cubes on the junk heap
raw materials for another creation
our languages mashed, these crumpled plans tossed

like pictures glossed by eternal rays of time

Louvered windows shade springtime days
Felt tips wet, roller-balls prepped
The office shuffles papers and taps on keys
It's a Friday and Pat Benitar plays
We Belong.

4/7/17

Repeat the Words Until True

I'm not one to stare at clouds
But today they stared at me
Buds of hate, punches vaporized
As a horse stretched into Figueroa
And had the north consumed by a boa

My pockets are empty

Days swirl in my coffee cup
Like Gentiles and Jews through the train station
Currents of words merge into waves
The sea of faces, too high to see above
In the echoed cadence of railway announcements

I can't hear it all

As I grow out my hair, my thoughts get smaller
In molded plastic parts with decals
Snap together. No cement if you rush
I paint them black with a broad brush
1/49th to scale

I sold everything

Soiled solo soul so still
Trying to become a poem
But rather a verse of words
A stuffed purse of billets and IOUs
A foot filling nothing but an empty shoe

I pretend I want to see you

7/18/17

Poem 2: Unlace my shoe

The sluts the butts the ruts the mutts
Candy colored wrinkles in Vivarin neon
Whispers from a peon and his dog Ed
When will he say what his eyes have said. Ha!
They say he died of flagellation
Maybe his back withheld salvation
Maybe not

Ya vremyoo trachoo.

3/27/94

this side of 24 years

the sluts, the butts
the ruts, the mutts
candy colored wrinkles in Vivarin neon
she said i was a peon, but no
instead she stretches bare breasted
knowing it's easy to mold me
in the motel, old carpets folded at the corners.
i don't think of our bed where
untold waves of passion and cold shoulders
blurring in layers of memory foam
washed up as flotsam on salty shores

we slide in starched cotton valleys
until all are left of us are outlines
crossed by power lines pointing towards lost horizons
a TV show echoes under cottage cheese skies
as my mind sinks in feelings of losing a shoe
but you are already dressed and pacing
facing lined curtains gently swaying in the breeze of the AC

in distant towns i wander sidewalks shirtless
stumbling through dry ditches
shuffling dirt streets lit by gaslights
a dog sees me and slips in an alley
two stars gawk from on high and i blink in their stare
the air brightens to blinding
your face appears, a white sign saying

"that's all, that's all," as i sink into your thighs

i awake alone with no other pill to take
marks on my back from your flagellation
the motel turns and withholds salvation
naked in my envelope i am returned to maker
two musty sinks drip rusty weakness
and peace slides in curved reflections by the tube TV
all memory blurs in these rises and falls
your fading face, a white sign saying
that's all, that's all.

(yes i wasted time)

mar 27-94 to feb 26-18

<u>your pledge of allegiance</u>

i pledge allegiance to beds in a bag
from the sweatshop children of Banglachina
and to non-stick cookware for which they stand (16 hours)
for one marketplace under LOL OMG
unprosecutable with slavery and products for all.

4/25/18

<u>this land is your land</u>

America, you mother,
you gave me nothing, now you take it all
waiting for another apology (to prove your flat earth topology)
with scientology stars trying to run the show.
i slip under crawl spaces, between your safe spaces
ready to brawl your so-called social graces
with f-bombs bigger than Kim Jong's atom bombs
shooting off more words than rounds from my room at the Mandalay
you can't make me stop. i'm locked and loaded
and i'm taking aim.

i was raised in hunting blinds behind white pickets
in places lighted by limbic fright and internet algorithms
where thick black faces carry guns shaped like cellphones
where rifles parade in streets before lead-poisoned homes
where Russian trolls call on conservative Jesus and the second amendment
this is not a celebrity speech for my commencement.
i am not a box to tick in one of your racial categories.

don't try to commodify me, consume me,
ply me with money and package me like food,
i see your apathy, unsympathy, always doing the rude thing
(when nobody's watching)
choosing a PR campaign and handshakes and printed lines (all lies).
i am not in the mood to make nice.
years have passed in corporate halls, and i'm sick of it all
with your credit scores and hordes of fantasy football whores
ready to kick those protesting on their knees. (right Yeezy?)
i'm outside the final Fosters Freeze waiting for it to thaw.

you'll hear this call whether you listen or not
like the time i cried out, jaundiced, barely nursed by dried milk.
you displayed a blade to make me behave,
to make me a slave in your money game,
your revisions of power plays, passion plays,
false parades of admiration and praise.
so i held up silk banners and gave you my days.
no, i have nothing good to say
and i will not shut up.

i hope you feel horrified for who i've become:
no longer a patriot, your favorite son,
your fan of open carry
(i give you salaam),
to march in prom suits before applause

to marry your cause of fakery and wrongs.
(where is my peace prize for dropping these bombs?)
this is not my country.
i do not belong.

beneath your floral pinafore
you store a history of pillage and rape
your gaping hole once shone in the sun
always calling, always fecund
you used to pose like the Statue of Liberty
but you took me in and never set me free
(slavery is a monster that makes monstrosities)
although i'm gone, you did what you intended
the teeth of these deep impressions still remain indented.

fuck you America. we see your lies and still eat Slim Jims from the QT
still buy dryer sheets and microbeads and Round Up
we all suffer you slippin' up
(look what i'm whippin' up).
i'm on Gucci.

5/9/18

<u>sunshine</u>

a song shines from his outline
sending out rays of sound
sidewalk eyes pause and slow time
they wait for this ray of divine
which flows between street signs with melody and tempo

we pretend to be mainly the same shape
just holes in space vibrating air
moving in set sequence on this flying ball
trained in increments towards ultimate expiration
all faced with outcomes of our animal brain

we're told to differentiate in our coffee choices
but true difference still remains
remnants of hidden stories told
pain, heroic gestures, beauty,
the main hallmark of (once) noble goals

i don't want to know the right kind of clothes,
which foods to eat at midnight
packaged consumption and national brands
your stand on TV shows
i want to see you shine like this surprise

in the street scene the song is done
standers disperse while some throw change
exchanges of thanks are strange and empty
missing the light beyond my shades
but at days dark end, every song fades.

6/22/18

<u>My Monstrosity</u>

There's a monster beneath my bed asking me for spare change, showing
receipts for a Greyhound ticket from last May as he wafts pungent BO
in my direction.
There's a monster in my closet speaking in tongues, prophesizing the
destruction of America by libtards while asking for tithes in a tan felt hat.
There's a monster in my chest begging for flesh and food and a retreat from
the eyes of men, all the while wishing he could dominate those who think
small with vicious charisma.
There's a monster in my head, magnifying flaws before burning them away
with concentrated light, his best work a constant thin whiff of white smoke.
There's a monster in my chemicals, hysterical and useless, its tentacles let
down a cloud of ink, a fog of insulin and dopamine as damp synapses shiver
in reply.
There's a monster in my ideas, fascist ideologues smack lecterns, never in turn
but a cacophony of absolutes clashing before the din of chanting pitchforks
and torches.
There's a monster on my soul, feeding off my final sparks of inspiration,
pressing me down until the aggravation to roll or move is just too much.
I know — you like it when I struggle.

My monsters swim naked in deep currents, arteries
Sparking dendrites, phantom limbs lost in some forgotten fight
Oxidized skies at the torn edge of firelight
I've prayed at their sacred sites,
Altars with bloody entrails, smoke and visceral delights
Faltering only after years of their awkward silence
This solo fight against resentment
Only results in these letters of spite
But monsters are wont to reply to such dull insight.

My monsters announce a war to end all wars
It comes with a theme song and a drop of colored flyers
Theorists on social media conspire to predict an outcome
But I'm already gone, a product of friendly fire
Dire warnings, like late night flashing traffic lights
Monsters always divine a way to be monstrous
And I am just meat for their perpetual carnage.

4/2/19

Medicinal

I learned to medicate
Making sensations to disrupt pain
When I lived in a cul-de-sac off Moeser Lane
Overlooking a small cluster of tall eucalyptus
Bark peeling, always a faint smell of antiseptic decay
From that postwar uphill suburban sprawl

I made movements, commuting across the Bay
Waiting in oily buses, always riding sideways
Every day was a journey alone
The grind of Muni engines, AC Transit engines, the roar of the Metro
While parents played out their own dramas
Throwing away any future that was mine

In *Descent into a Maelstrom*
I was the man in the barrel
But I was also the guttural hole, taking in everything
I had no words, no syllables, no utterance
Raised mute in the aorta
Struck dumb, left dumb, agape
The ache of an animal caged and pacing
Faces faked for the sake of faking

I learned to medicate, masticate,
Making sensations to disrupt pain
And I remained in stasis, stuck in my lane
In line at the toll gate waiting to pay for every mistake
The whine of hunger the only constant
As I became your hollow Easter egg

You feigned interest, offered a shrug
(You don't need to placate)
Saying you loved the space in me
Big enough for you to hide your mistakes
As my pieces laid in currents, frothing waves on the shore
The coldness of the bay, a grateful numbness.

4/11/19

Passing M-Day

I never scratched like this before
These dry heaves of creativity
From what used to be a brimming store
My reason for breathing is changing
And I'm no longer bleeding
Thankless and rankled by perfect oppression
I am post trauma
Cleaning up years of rubble from my demolition

Out of the gate you hobbled me
Dependent on your drug-like attention
Believing the lies you told your royal "we"
Days spent in front of the TV
Shackled and thinking I was free
Entitled to be great simply by your decree

You always tipped my scales in your favor
Your performances,
Parades, I was a float for your attention
Decorated, hollow,
With all your hot air gone
I collapsed under my own weight

Your painted skies – only a ceiling
Window dressings of feelings
Your pew kneelings just a means for your own praise
While prostrate alkaline plants stress on the upright piano
Water rings, white memories
You covered them in embroidered stories

In the mid-morning, the mist yet uncleared
You echo from across the fallow field
Telling me how to stand and walk and be
Repeated as you approach to become larger with me
But I keep distance to make you small, if there at all
Just an itch that begs for scratching
Your white roots showing
Self-congratulation poised on pursed lips
Platitudes and propaganda
Pausing for someone to give you a hand.

5/12/19

The Conclusion

Always see the end in the beginning
You told me from the start
Two coffees steaming in ceramic
One shoulder bare
You said it was too warm in the sound of Miles Davis
But I rested on a cusp that left a permanent impression

In the years it's taken for you to hate me
I dug myself in
Just a mole burrowing in damp darkness
Sniffing my way through pleasure and pain

Or maybe I was a hermit crab claws extended
Scuttling sideways on vulnerable shores
Ready at a moment's notice to retreat into my shell
Just a shield for my soft true form

In my distance from you
I assumed monstrous proportions
And you flew your flag of lies
Both of us longing for our mutual demise

I've seen dry flotsam of many seas on rough sand
The bland décor of corporate acceptability
Thrumming fluorescent vibrations tinting thirsty visions
This is just a revision of another decade gone
The final chords in the conclusion of this song
Where you sang the dissonant melody.
My cells have cycled and recycled
But senescence is setting in
And so I crystallize into my final body

I tried to explain through codes and codices
Though slim and lacking in vigor
They still contain my muscle and bone
In the sinews and thews, the skein of words
This conversation feigns a convincing conversion
An inversion of beautiful grotesqueries
Fitting to end this pain and suffering
Your eyes will determine the value they bring

This is our swansong of hatred and loss

The cost of a thousand missteps and resentment
Bitter edged incisions in what was once clueless flesh
These days you remain mute with back turned
Shoulders hunched and put away
Grey thoughts rolling off you in waves

They say death is a painful end
But it seems more like a weight released
The knife, a relief
A peace beyond hunger and want
Where I transition to become that mole
A fitting end for my clouded soul
Blinded and unreminded
An obscure sliver of life left to scrape
Remaining days without rays of light
In soft layers of endless organic decay.

6/5/19

www.ingramcontent.com/pod-product-compliance
Lightning Source LLC
LaVergne TN
LVHW041207080426
835508LV00008B/845